WHY A
REVERSE
MORTGAGE?

NICK
WE APPRECIATE YOUR
PAST REFERRALS AND
THOUGHT MY NEW BOOK
MIGHT INTEREST YOU
OR A FRIEND.

11/23/21

WHY A
REVERSE
MORTGAGE?

Real-life Success Stories

DON OPEKA
NMLS 261505

WHY A
REVERSE
MORTGAGE?

Published by
Illumify Media Global
www.IllumifyMedia.com
"Let's bring your book to life!"

Library of Congress Control Number: 2021914952

Paperback ISBN: 978-1-955043-12-0
eBook ISBN: 978-1-955043-13-7

Typeset by Art Innovations (http://artinnovations.in/)
Cover design by Debbie Lewis

Printed in the United States of America

CONTENTS

ACKNOWLEDGEMENTS

Although he passed in 2019, I have to acknowledge the contributions Joe Sabah made by constantly encouraging me to "Sing the Song I was Made to Sing."

This book would not have happened without the work and encouragement of both my wife, Terri, and Amanda Varga. Amanda did the important work of translating my initial thoughts into readable form.

I must also acknowledge the comments, help, and encouragement I received from the early readers of my manuscript. Each one helped to improve the book. Their comments were a great encouragement.

EARLY READER COMMENTS

Early readers were not asked to put their name on the comments.

"Appears to be a good method for retired persons to leverage their most valuable asset. Probably ideal for those with insufficient retirement savings."

"A Reverse Mortgage can be useful in many more ways than I thought"

"It can be a great method financially to use your asset to stay at home"

"I already have a Reverse Mortgage, and I think this is a wonderful product that all eligible adults should consider!"

"It gave me peace of mind knowing that I understand more clearly what a Reverse Mortgage was."

"I feel although it is not for everyone, a Reverse Mortgage is something that all of aging adults can certainly benefit from"

"I wouldn't say surprised me as much as how much I thought I knew but didn't! The distribution options were enlightening."

"They are a wonderful tool when used appropriately."

"Enjoyed reading your manuscript. This will be very helpful for those in the senior housing industry."

"Made it much more understandable. I am example oriented and the various stories brought it home."

"Don – you did a great job on this. This needs to replace the old "Use Your Home to Stay at Home" booklet we have to send out!" (This comment from a Reverse Mortgage counselor)

INTRODUCTION

A dissectologist is a person who enjoys assembling jigsaw puzzles. A Reverse Mortgage Loan Originator is a person who helps his clients assemble their financial picture. For both the dissectologist and the loan originator, the idea is to bring the various pieces together to form a complete picture, not to view them in isolation. Throughout this book, I will help you explore how a Reverse Mortgage can fit into a larger financial picture for homeowners with diverse histories and goals.

Consider the case of a woman who decided to take advantage of a Reverse Mortgage to complete her financial picture after losing her job at age eighty-two. She was working with other pieces: a fixed income, monthly mortgage payments, credit card payments, and deferred home maintenance. By bringing the Reverse Mortgage piece into play, she eliminated her monthly mortgage and credit card payments and completed her home repairs. She added guaranteed monthly income for as long as she lives in her home. I will provide more details in Chapter 2, but please consider that a Reverse Mortgage is not a one-size-fits-all solution as you settle in for a short read. Depending on the situation, it may eliminate monthly mortgage payments, increase income, or both.

As I sit here today, putting the finishing touches on this book, I am seventy-five years old and have been in the mortgage business with my wife, Terri, for twenty-five years. We have built not just "client relationships" but true friendships with many of our borrowers. As our business has shifted to include Reverse Mortgage loans, the urgency of sharing what we have seen and experienced has grown exponentially. I have often found that discussing this topic in an email, or even a conversation, does not provide enough context. There are many other books on this topic that describe the technical aspects of these loans. I specifically wrote this book from my perspective, that of a loan originator who has conversations with every borrower and remains in contact with many borrowers years after the loan closes.

My goal with this book is to *educate* potential borrowers, their families, and professionals who work with seniors; *share* some of the life-changing stories of these loans; and *encourage* everyone to become knowledgeable enough to make informed decisions. Thank you in advance for joining me on this journey!

Before we dive into the topic of Reverse Mortgages, I want to give you a bit of history, so you have a better understanding of who I am. Long before my career in the mortgage business, I graduated from Rensselaer Polytechnic Institute with an engineering degree, followed by military service as a pilot and plane commander in the US Navy. After four and a half years in the Navy, I worked as a sales engineer, selling natural gas compressors. In those days, I performed engineering calculations on a slide rule before getting my first calculator in 1975.

In 1980, I purchased a programmable calculator, which I programmed to suit my needs. Two years later, I bought my first computer with a word processor. Why is this relevant? In my younger years, I constantly pushed the envelope on new technology and could never understand the "old guys" who weren't interested in learning how to use these new devices. However, more than forty years later, I have *become* one of those "old guys" who finds the latest and greatest technology more annoying than helpful. As it turns out, many Reverse Mortgage borrowers no longer use computers, never had one in the first place, or do not use one with the ease of the younger generations. Quite frankly, many of these borrowers simply prefer doing business in person and on paper. The move toward automating the mortgage process through apps and call centers has taken the personal touch out of loan origination. While this may benefit traditional mortgages and tech-savvy applicants, I find that the Reverse Mortgage process benefits from a person-to-person approach.

After twenty-three years in sales for fifteen companies across three different industries, I left my last corporate job in 1996 when my wife and I launched our business, Orion Mortgage, Inc. We have been working together, and for ourselves, ever since. In 1996, there was little standardized training for anyone in the mortgage industry and no licensing requirements in Colorado. We learned our business one loan at a time by diligently pursuing both knowledge and opportunities. Soon we had a successful business based on repeat customers and word-of-mouth marketing. In 2006, when Colorado began requiring licenses for our profession, we both took the necessary steps to achieve licensure and have consistently maintained our status as Licensed Loan Originators ever since.

We have divided the tasks of bringing a borrower through the various steps of applying for, processing, and closing a loan to utilize each of our strengths to the greatest advantage. Most borrower conversations start with me. I walk the borrower through the entire loan application process. In this conversation, I discover their reasons for getting a loan, analyze the current situation, and offer solutions to help achieve current and future goals. Once a loan application is signed, Terri takes over the file and oversees the loan processing. She has regular contact with borrowers and answers their questions as they gather their necessary documents. She communicates with underwriters to ensure they have what they need to approve the loan and makes sure the appraisal process runs as smoothly as possible. After the underwriter has given the loan a "clear to close," the file goes back over to me, and I attend the closing with our borrower as the final loan documents are signed. Throughout these steps, Terri and I are constantly reviewing details, trying to foresee and address any potential concerns, and working together to structure the best possible loan for each of our borrowers. Technically, each of us *could* perform all the various functions throughout the loan process, but we each enjoy some parts more than others, and our temperaments are better suited to different roles. Our system must work because we have had a successful twenty-five years providing Colorado homeowners with loans!

During our first decade in business, we became aware of Reverse Mortgages, but since they were FHA products, we referred all prospects to others. We were committed to a low-cost business model, and the costs to originate FHA loans were prohibitive for a small company. In 2010, the rules changed to make it reasonable for us to originate FHA loans.

In 2011, a financial planner referred a gentleman for a traditional mortgage. At the time, he was seventy-seven years old, had sold a successful business, and seemed well-situated for retirement. Unfortunately, problems stemming from the sale of the business were threatening his retirement. The buyer of his business had not refinanced the business loan into his name and had stopped making payments. The business loan still had our borrower's home as collateral, which meant the bank threatened to foreclose on his home.

Originally, this borrower came to us for a traditional cash-out refinance to pay off the bank so he could repossess his old business. The problem was that since he was no longer the *owner* of the business, he did not have the documentable income necessary to qualify for the refinance. After reviewing his total situation, I recommended that he apply for a Reverse Mortgage, which he *did* qualify for. His Reverse Mortgage provided the cash he needed to pay off the bank. He was able to recover the business assets and began the process of selling them off.

We started originating Reverse Mortgages to solve a borrower's problem. As we have continued to help borrowers, we have seen how powerful this product can be when properly applied.

In these next chapters, I will be describing the products and processes in ways intended to cover transactions as they are done in Colorado. I am not attempting to cover all the technical details or explain every nuance. I am not a lawyer and do not provide legal advice. I recommend that if you have any legal questions about a specific transaction that you consult a lawyer. For the latest rules and technical data concerning FHA-insured Reverse Mortgages, see: https://www.hud.gov/program_offices/housing/sfh/hecm.

For the sake of consistency, I will use the terms "borrower" or "client" in the singular even though there may be, and often are, two borrowers in a Reverse Mortgage transaction. I am using the pronoun "she" for both the sake of consistency for the reader and because single borrowers tend to be female more often than not.

You will find terms defined in the glossary at the back of the book.

REVERSE MORTGAGE BASICS

A Reverse Mortgage is a loan that provides access to a portion of a home's value through options suited to the borrower's needs. The term "Reverse Mortgage" comes from the concept of receiving payments *from* a lender instead of making payments *to* a lender. You may hear the term "HECM" (pronounced heck-um) within the mortgage industry, which is the acronym for Home Equity Conversion Mortgage. This is the proper name for an FHA-insured Reverse Mortgage. For the sake of simplicity, this book uses the term "Reverse Mortgage" rather than "HECM."

Most people are understandably confused by the idea of having a home loan that does not require monthly mortgage payments. With a Reverse Mortgage, the only mortgage payment required is when the borrower no longer lives in the house due to a *decision* to move, *placement* in a care community, or *death*. This single required payment pays off the loan by satisfying repayment of the principal loan amount, all accrued interest, and any additional fees. Between the time the loan is originated and when the loan comes due, interest is accruing on the unpaid balance. This interest accrual is why a Reverse Mortgage borrower cannot access 100 percent of her value and why the final payment to satisfy the loan will typically be higher than the original principal loan amount. (See Appendix Table A in the back of the book for a chart and explanation.)

The Principal Limit calculation is determined by the government, based on the interest rate, and the age of the borrower. This dictates how much of the property value is available to the borrower and how much is to account for the accrual of interest and other costs over the life of the loan. The goal of these calculations is to have equity remaining in the house when the loan comes due. The actual tables for an FHA Reverse Mortgage can be accessed at: https://www.hud.gov/program_offices/housing/sfh/hecm. FHA also limits the amount of the Principal Limit a borrower can access in the first year.

As with any other home loan, the lender does not own the home. The lender has a lien against the property, as evidenced by a Note and a Deed of Trust. The loan is a contract that commits both the lender and the borrower to certain responsibilities. The primary responsibilities of the borrower in a Reverse Mortgage contract are to:

1. Live in the home as a Primary Residence,
2. Pay—on time and in full—all property taxes, homeowner's insurance, any HOA (Homeowners Association) dues,
3. Maintain the property to FHA standards, and
4. Pay off the loan by the sale of the property, refinance, or cash from other resources when the loan comes due.

With a traditional forward mortgage, tax and insurance payments are often made through an escrow account. It is common for a Reverse Mortgage borrower to be responsible for making those payments directly to the appropriate entity. If a borrower does not have a history of making tax and insurance payments on time and in full, or if the borrower prefers to know that those payments are coming through the lender, then there is a provision called a Life Expectancy Set Aside or LESA. The funds for these payments will be calculated based on anticipated costs and borrower age and deducted from the borrower's available funds. Note that if the funds that are set aside to pay taxes and insurance are exhausted, the borrower will be required to pay these from other resources.

The Life Expectancy Set Aside is just one way to personalize a Reverse Mortgage to the needs and preferences of each borrower. It cannot be stressed enough that a Reverse Mortgage is not a one-size-fits-all loan product. A loan originator who has the borrower's best interest in mind and takes the time to understand the borrower's current situation and future goals will help structure a Reverse Mortgage to the borrower's greatest advantage.

Many FHA Reverse Mortgages have an adjustable interest rate. However, for some borrowers, a fixed-rate loan is preferable. Interest rates on any fixed-rate Reverse Mortgage are likely to be higher than on a traditional forward mortgage. With a traditional forward mortgage, the loan balance is going down with time, so the lender's risk is also going down with time. With a fixed-rate Reverse Mortgage, the loan balance is going up with time as interest accrues. This factor increases the risk for the lender, which translates to higher rates. With a fixed-rate Reverse Mortgage, all proceeds are distributed at closing, and interest accrual commences immediately.

The distribution options for an adjustable-rate FHA Reverse Mortgage are as follows:

Lump Sum: This is the term used when the borrower makes a single withdrawal from her available Principal Limit. The borrower may choose to take out a portion of her proceeds at closing or later in the life of her loan. If there is an existing mortgage to be paid off, the payoff will be part of the initial lump-sum distribution.

Tenure Payment: This is one of the unique features of a Reverse Mortgage and is an ideal option for a borrower who wishes to reliably supplement her income long-term. When a borrower chooses this option, she receives a guaranteed payment from the mortgage every month for as long as she lives in the house and complies with other loan terms. An FHA calculation bases the payment amount on available Principal Limit, expected interest rate, and age.

Term Payment: The dollar amount for term payments is selected by the borrower rather than based on the FHA calculation. Working within the amount of money available, these payments can be stopped, restarted, increased, or decreased as the borrower desires. Unlike a tenure payment, these payments are not guaranteed to continue as long as the borrower lives in the house. Term payments will stop when the available Principal Limit has been used or when the borrower chooses, whichever comes first. *If all of the available Principal Limit is used, the borrower still owns the house, and she can still re-*

side in the house as long as she complies with other loan requirements. She simply does not have additional money to tap into from this loan. She will not have a mandatory mortgage payment until the loan comes due. She still has to pay taxes, insurance, and maintenance.

Line of Credit: As with a home equity line of credit (HELOC) or a credit card, this option means an amount of money can be accessed whenever the borrower wants to. With a Reverse Mortgage line of credit, the available funds typically will grow over time. This growth is based on the difference between the loan balance and the Principal Limit even if the borrower accesses some of the funds. (See Appendix Table A.) This is a point to discuss with a loan originator and may be a reason to choose a higher rate rather than the lowest rate on a Reverse Mortgage. As with the term payment option, if all the available funds from the line of credit have been used, the borrower still owns her home and does not have to make a mortgage payment until the loan comes due. She does have to pay taxes, insurance, and maintenance.

While a HELOC draw period typically ends after ten years, the line of credit draw period (time allowed to withdraw money from the line of credit) on an FHA Reverse Mortgage extends for the life of the loan. However, as with the lump sum distribution option, FHA does limit the amount of money available in a line of credit for the first year after obtaining a Reverse Mortgage. This limit will be shown in the proposal, application, and closing documents.

Combination: One of the most under-appreciated aspects of a Reverse Mortgage is the ability to utilize as many, or few, of these options as the borrower needs *and* the ability to change the options during the life of the loan. For example, suppose a borrower originally decides to have her available Principal Limit distributed as tenure payments but later wants a lump sum of cash. In that case, she can take the lump sum withdrawal and have her tenure payments recalculated based on the new difference between the loan balance and Principal Limit. The payments will be smaller but still guaranteed for as long as she lives in her home.

Making Payments: While not a distribution option, many borrowers overlook the opportunity to
make payments to reduce their Reverse Mortgage
loan balance. As explained earlier, no mortgage
payment is ever required until the loan comes due,
but the option to pay down the balance of a Reverse
Mortgage is available at any time during the life of
the loan. For instance, if a Reverse Mortgage has
a line of credit, any payments the borrower makes
to pay down the balance owed will increase the
amount available from the line of credit and can be
accessed later if desired. If the loan is a fixed rate,
payments will reduce the balance and interest accrual, but there will be no ability to access the money later without refinancing the loan.

We have all heard that if something sounds too
good to be true, it usually is. We are all suspicious
of a catch. With a Reverse Mortgage, the "catch" for
some people is the FHA Mortgage Insurance. For a
traditional forward loan, borrowers with less than 20
percent equity typically must pay for mortgage insurance. This protects the lender if the borrower de-
faults on the loan, leaving the lender with no choice

but to foreclose. A forward mortgage borrower with more than 20 percent equity should be able to sell the property and receive cash at closing, eliminating the need for foreclosure. Borrowers with more equity in their homes are less likely to be required to have mortgage insurance on a forward loan. *For an FHA Reverse Mortgage, mortgage insurance plays a much larger role and protects both the borrower and the lender.*

FHA Mortgage Insurance protects the borrower in the following ways:

1. Guarantee of funds for a line of credit: When a Reverse Mortgage borrower utilizes the line of credit option, these funds are guaranteed to be available regardless of changes in the economy or the lender going out of business. If you think back to what happened in 2008–2009, many banks and credit unions canceled or reduced home equity lines of credit (HELOCs) because of financial stress at the bank. These institutions had the authority to cut off a borrower from her funds. If the borrower had opted for a

Reverse Mortgage instead of a HELOC, she still could have accessed her line of credit. This is why the federal guarantee of FHA Mortgage Insurance is important for Reverse Mortgages. A borrower choosing a Reverse Mortgage line of credit at age sixty-two expects the line of credit to be available when she is 102 (if she has not spent it, of course), so it should be properly insured and as secure as a bank deposit as long as the borrower complies with the loan terms.

2. Guarantee of funds for tenure or other payments: When a Reverse Mortgage borrower utilizes the tenure payment option, these payment amounts are based on available Principal Limit, expected interest rate, and the borrower's age. The goal of the calculation is to have the loan balance lower than the property value when the loan comes due. However, if the borrower outlives her estimated life expectancy, the tenure payments are still guaranteed to continue,

even if the total value of the payments exceeds the home's value. Term payments are similarly guaranteed, up to the Principal Limit, as long as the borrower complies with the loan terms.

3. Non-recourse loan: FHA mortgage insurance guarantees the only collateral for the loan is the home. If the value of the home is not adequate to pay off the loan, FHA will pay the short. There cannot be a claim against other borrower assets.

Consider an example of a sixty-five-year-old woman who structures her Reverse Mortgage so that she begins receiving tenure payments right away. We will call her Mary. Now let us assume that Mary is genetically blessed, takes good care of herself, lives to 105, and has stayed in her home for all of those years. The total amount of the guaranteed monthly payments over forty years has most likely exceeded her home's value when the loan originated. However, because of the FHA Mortgage Insurance, Mary's payments were faithfully continued even when the total she had received was greater than the home value. A US government guarantee is imperative to the success of this loan product.

If you think that being in your home at 105 is a stretch, we have originated a Reverse Mortgage for a woman who was 104 at the time of her loan. She was living in the first home that she and her husband had purchased together decades earlier. More on that story later.

FHA mortgage insurance also protects the *lender* by "paying the shortage." In our example of Mary, who opted for a tenure payment that continued well past her statistical life expectancy, FHA mortgage insurance protects the lender in addition to the borrower. When Mary passes away or moves out of her house, if she owes more money on the loan than the house is worth at the time of her moving out, the lender does not have the right to pursue her estate or her heirs to pay for the difference. Instead, FHA covers the shortage. This comes into play when *any* FHA Reverse Mortgage borrower is finished with the house and the loan comes due. A house may be worth a significant amount of money at the start of a loan, enabling a borrower to tap into hundreds of thousands of dollars, but at the end of the loan, due to some unforeseen shift in the local housing market, the home might be worth much less. In this instance, the FHA mortgage insurance would cover the difference between what the house is worth when the loan is paid off and how much was taken out over the life of the loan.

How can the lender not go after the borrower, heirs, or estate for the short on the loan if the home value has dropped? This is yet another powerful feature of Reverse Mortgages. FHA Reverse Mortgages are non-recourse loans. In simple terms, this means that the only collateral for the loan is the house, and the only thing the lender has a right to is the house. The lender has no recourse against, or right to access, any other property or assets the borrower may have while living or after she has died. Consider what that means for adult children.

Let us return to the hypothetical example of Mary. She remained in her home by accessing part of her home value through a Reverse Mortgage and setting up tenure payments. She was fortunate enough to stay in her home until she passed away at 105 years of age. Her children, knowing the house is worth less than is owed on the loan, have the option of simply leaving the lender to deal with the house. The lender has no right to Mary's art collection, has no business finding out what her investments are worth, and cannot put any sort of lien against the rest of the estate. Her heirs may choose to simply turn the keys over to the lender and move forward with their lives. FHA has a "Cash for Keys" program that can provide cash to the family in return for avoiding a foreclosure action. Contact the mortgage servicer listed on the monthly mortgage statement about this option.

What if the house Mary had lived in for all those years is important to the family and they want to keep it, but the loan balance is greater than the home value? *Then* do they have to pay the loan back in full? No. *The borrower, heirs, or estate will never owe more than the house value when the loan comes due.* If the heirs want to keep the property, they will have to pay for an FHA appraisal and pay 95 percent of that appraised value to the lender to satisfy the loan. The house will be theirs, and the FHA mortgage insurance covers the difference between what they paid and what is owed to the lender to satisfy the original loan. The borrower/heirs/estate decides whether to walk away or keep the house, not the lender.

Regardless of the circumstances surrounding the loan coming due—a borrower choosing to move, needing community care placement, or her death—she or her heirs will never have to pay the difference between the value of the home at the time she leaves it and the balance due on the loan if the loan balance is greater than the home value. However, if the home's value is greater than the balance due on the loan, the proceeds of the sale remaining after the loan is paid in full go to the borrower or her heirs.

Important note: If Mary was on Medicaid, then Medicaid may have a claim against the estate, which may cause part or all of the proceeds of the home sale to go to Medicaid.

The non-recourse feature is important here because, based on early reader feedback, some borrowers or their heirs have unnecessarily taken mon-ey to closing when the home was sold. This can happen if the sale price is not adequate to pay off the loan and the seller does not raise the non-re-course issue. Closing agents do not routinely inves-tigate the terms of a loan being paid off. They just ask for a payoff amount from the servicer. The ser-vicer provides the payoff but typically has no idea of what the sale price or terms are. If the result is a closing that requires cash from the seller, it is up to the seller to point out the non-recourse feature to avoid paying the difference.

Many prospective borrowers who have no chil-dren plan to let the lender have the home. This is also a disservice because many homes will have hundreds of thousands of dollars of equity when the loan comes due. If there are no heirs, it would be better to make arrangements for the equity to go to a church, charity, or other non-profit organization than to have it lost to an unnecessary foreclosure. Remember that no lender ever wants to foreclose a house. They want the money they lend back with interest. All Reverse Mortgages are structured with the intent by the lender to have enough equity when the loan comes due so the borrower, their heirs, or another party will sell the home, pay off the loan, and walk away with cash. Any foreclosure results in a disappointed lender.

Considering all the protective aspects of FHA Mortgage Insurance, why is it sometimes viewed as "the catch" to a Reverse Mortgage? Simply put: because it looks expensive. When a borrower understands the value of the protection, the cost is easily justified. However, if all a potential borrower considers is the dollar figure in the line item for "mortgage insurance" on her loan proposal package, it can be a bit shocking. The up-front mortgage insurance on a Reverse Mortgage is currently 2 percent of the property value, up to a maximum lendable value of $822,375. This is often more than the total of all other closing costs, but the expense can be rolled into the loan. On a $500,000 house, the up-front mortgage insurance would be $10,000, and the monthly accrual (not *paid* monthly but *accruing* monthly against the balance of the loan to be paid at the end of the loan along with principal and interest) would be 0.5 percent per year of the loan balance (cal-culated monthly). On a HECM-to-HECM refinance (the refinancing of an existing Reverse Mortgage to a new Reverse Mortgage), there is a calculation to give the borrower credit for the mortgage insurance already paid on the first Reverse Mortgage.

The fact that monthly accruals will be calculated based on the loan's balance is important enough to highlight again. A borrower should understand that her loan balance is going up every month if she chooses not to make payments. (See Appendix.) Mortgage insurance, interest, and possibly a service fee are being added to the principal balance each month. This is the reason why a Reverse Mortgage borrower cannot access 100 percent of the home's value at closing. A portion of the value she does not have access to at closing is set aside for accrual of interest, mortgage insurance, and any other charg-es. The borrower does not have to make a payment each month to cover these costs because they are accruing against the loan balance. *This does mean that the amount owed when the loan comes due will normally be more than the initial amount borrowed.*

The accumulating monthly mortgage insurance and interest against the principal will all come due, in full, when the borrower leaves the house (or, in the case of more than one borrower, when the *last* borrower leaves the house) or when the loan is in default due to non-compliance. If this concept is not fully explained and understood, a borrower or her heirs may be upset that there is less money available after the home's sale than had been anticipated. The bottom line here is that once you spend home value—either as loan principal or as costs accrued over time—you cannot expect to have that home value transformed into cash when the house sells. *Is it possible that due to a rise in home values, there will be more equity at the end of the loan than was anticipated?* Of course! But there is no guarantee of that happening.

What if a borrower wants to keep the costs at the end of the loan to a minimum? She can make occasional or regular payments against the accruing costs and/or the principal balance if she chooses to do so. The key here is that it is a *choice*. A Reverse Mortgage borrower is not required to make any mortgage payments during her loan. Yes, she must pay taxes, insurance, HOA dues, and maintain her home, but she does not have to pay the lender until she no longer lives in the house. If the borrower wants to pay her monthly mortgage insurance and interest, she can. If the borrower comes into an inheritance and wants to pay down her balance, she can. I recommend paying the loan *down* but not paying it *off* if it is an adjustable-rate Reverse Mortgage. The difference? Paying it off will close the loan entirely, and if the borrower wants to tap into her line of credit again, she will have to start all over with a new loan. If she pays the loan balance *down* and keeps the loan open, she will have easy access to her line of credit at any time.

This is what Terri and I have done with our Reverse Mortgage. We keep the loan balance low but don't pay it off completely. What are the advantages of this? First, our Reverse Mortgage is in place, and we have access to a growing line of credit if we should have a need for money. Second, if we were to sell our house, we would only owe a few hundred dollars to our Reverse Mortgage lender to satisfy the loan. The freedom and peace of mind offered by both features are immeasurable. How long can we maintain this? We were both sixty-two or older when we originated our loan, and this loan will be in place until we refinance, move, have both passed away, or when Terri, who is several years younger than me, turns 150. *Every loan must have a due date, and FHA sets the due date for a Reverse Mortgage at 150 years of age (for the youngest borrower) so that the likelihood of anyone being "aged out" of their loan is infinitesimal.* The realistic and anticipated end of a Reverse Mortgage is when the last borrower moves or dies. I expect we have a long way to go on our Reverse Mortgage. You might be wondering why I made the point about our ages. Let me explain.

Age is one of the loan-qualification conditions. For an FHA Reverse Mortgage, at least one borrower must be sixty-two or older. The calculation mentioned earlier that determines how much of the home's value can be accessed is always based on the *youngest* borrower's age. If one spouse is under sixty-two, they must be included on the loan as a "Qualified Non-Borrowing Spouse." This protects the younger spouse from the loan coming due and a possible foreclosure if the older spouse dies. The Qualified Non-Borrowing Spouse may remain in the home if she abides by the loan conditions, including paying taxes, insurance, and maintenance. However, only a borrower can access funds in a line of credit, and if the borrower passes away, the non-borrowing spouse will not be able to access any remaining funds. *If marriage happens after a Reverse Mortgage is in place, a refinance is required to add a new spouse to the loan. If the loan is not refinanced to add the new spouse, the loan will come due when the borrowing spouse leaves the home.*

What are the other loan requirements? A few have been mentioned already. The borrower must pay her taxes, insurance, HOA dues, and maintain her home. At the beginning of the loan, the FHA maintenance standards can be a bit prickly for some people. This is addressed in Chapter 3. In addition, a borrower can only get a Reverse Mortgage on her primary residence. Being a snowbird or owning

a vacation home or rental properties are not problems, but the only property eligible for a Reverse
Mortgage is the one the borrower lives in for the
majority of the year. This is typically where she files
her taxes and is registered to vote. If a borrower
needs to leave her primary residence temporarily
for a hospital stay or rehabilitation services, this will
not trigger the loan to come due as long as the intent is for her to return home.

The final factor to consider is the borrower's ability
to qualify for the loan based on income, assets, and
credit. While the threshold for these requirements is
set fairly low, that threshold still needs to be met or
exceeded. Unfortunately, some potential borrowers
reach out too late. Some people—borrowers, family
members, and professionals alike—view Reverse
Mortgages as a loan of last resort. Many of these
individuals think this way because they do not fully
understand the loan product or have heard negative stories about Reverse Mortgages. *Regardless
of why they think this way, the myth that Reverse
Mortgages are only for poor people or should only
be used if all else fails causes many seniors to leave*

this option unexplored as they navigate the finances of their retirement years.

Many potential borrowers think that if they can get a loan today, it will be available later too. This is wrong. One flaw in this thinking is that a borrower's ability to qualify for the loan may change suddenly. Many people who qualify for a Reverse Mortgage are still working and not ready to stop. Unfortunately, health issues, job layoffs, or other unexpected changes (like COVID) can reduce income. A person may have planned to wait longer before receiving Social Security but may find that without it, she no longer has the income to qualify for a Reverse Mortgage, just when one might be the most helpful. Another flaw in the "I'll do it later" mentality is that FHA can change the guidelines and pricing at any time and with little to no warning, which has happened in the past. Borrowers who qualify for a Reverse Mortgage before a rule change do not necessarily qualify after the rule change.

This is particularly important to consider for commissioned or self-employed people who plan to work beyond age sixty-two. Some may find their working years end before they are financially ready, and others continue working for many years beyond their contemporaries. If a borrower is still in a financial position to make regular mortgage payments, she can make payments to reduce her Reverse Mortgage balance just like a traditional forward mortgage. When her situation changes, she can decrease or stop making payments, or even begin taking payments *from* the Reverse Mortgage. There would be no need to request forbearance, a temporary decrease or pause in mortgage payments, as some homeowners did during COVID, if a Reverse Mortgage was in place.

Another concern for borrowers hoping to qualify for a Reverse Mortgage is too much credit card debt. Reverse Mortgage guidelines may or may not allow a borrower to use loan proceeds to pay down debt to qualify for the loan. In one case, a married couple qualified for a Reverse Mortgage but had to make home repairs to meet FHA guidelines before closing the loan. The husband, a contractor, planned to do the work himself. By the time the work was complete, the couple's credit card debt

had increased to the point that they no longer qualified for the loan. Instead of a Reverse Mortgage,
they refinanced into a VA debt consolidation loan.
If the borrowers make payments on time and do
not build up additional debt, they might qualify for
a Reverse Mortgage after one year. *Some contrac-
tors are willing to make necessary repairs before
the loan closing and receive payment from the loan
proceeds.*

What are some of the misunderstandings that
might cause someone to *not* consider a Reverse
Mortgage? Here are the top five *myths* and corre-
sponding truths about Reverse Mortgages:

1. *The lender owns the home.* This is the most
   common misconception about Reverse
   Mortgages. The fact is, the borrower owns
   the home. The borrower may choose to sell,
   refinance, or pay off her Reverse Mortgage,
   just like she could with a traditional forward
   mortgage. The borrower must comply with
   the terms of her loan so she is not in default,
   but that is the same as any other home
   loan.

2. *The home must be free and clear of all mortgages.* An easy, although not precise, way to look at the possibility of getting a Reverse Mortgage on a house with an existing loan is that a borrower at age sixty-two should owe less than half of the home's value. An older borrower can owe more. The exact calculation is based on the Principal Limit Tables published at <u>hud.gov</u>, but your Reverse Mortgage originator will do the calculation for you. In certain circumstances, a borrower may choose to bring cash to close for a Reverse Mortgage. A recently widowed borrower cared for her special-needs adult child in her home. The security of knowing she would not have to make a mortgage payment was important enough for her to bring cash to pay the Mandatory Obligations down to the Principal Limit. This was an effective way to use her husband's life insurance proceeds.

3. *The borrower is restricted on how to use the loan proceeds.* It is not unusual to discuss

that a Reverse Mortgage is a way to fund in-home care, home renovations for safety and accessibility, Medicare copays and deductibles, and ease up the finances while one spouse cares for another. However, a borrower does not have to use loan proceeds for these "practical" uses. A borrower may use the proceeds however she sees fit—dream vacations, a new vehicle, an investment property, etc., just as with any other cash-out refinance. Much to the chagrin of many adult children, a Reverse Mortgage borrower has the right to spend loan proceeds without her children's permission or approval. Adult children, an executor, or another trusted advisor should be aware of the decision to get a Reverse Mortgage. The purpose of this is not to approve or disapprove but rather to have someone else in the loop if the borrower declines in her ability to make decisions or is at risk of being taken advantage of by a third party. Proper planning now can make life easier later.

4. *The loan proceeds are taxed.* Simply false—Reverse Mortgage payments to borrowers are not taxed because they are distributions of loan proceeds instead of income.

5. *Only poor people need Reverse Mortgages.* Borrowers on Medicaid can receive Reverse Mortgages, and they are also useful for borrowers with substantial assets. These latter borrowers are generally referred to a loan originator because a financial advisor has crunched the numbers and realized that this loan product would be the most cost-effective way to free up some cash. For higher net worth individuals, some questions to consider are: Is it better to use money from a Reverse Mortgage or take an early withdrawal from an annuity that may involve early termination fees and taxes? Is it better to take money from a tax-sheltered investment account and pay taxes on the money before making a mortgage payment or to get a Reverse Mortgage and eliminate the need to pay taxes before making

a mortgage payment? Can a Reverse Mortgage provide cash instead of liquidating rapidly appreciating assets or assets in a depressed market? Can a Reverse Mortgage provide liquidity for a person with substantial business or other high-value assets that are not liquid? In many cases, a Reverse Mortgage is one choice of many, rather than a product to be considered in isolation. There are many potential borrowers between the extremes of Medicaid recipients and multi-millionaires who could benefit from having a Reverse Mortgage in place.

2 THE STORIES

Borrower stories best explain the concepts behind Reverse Mortgages and the importance
of spreading the word about this exceptionally
underutilized financial tool. It is crucial to understand
that a Reverse Mortgage is just that, *a tool*, one of many
that should be in every senior's financial toolbox. An
even better analogy is to see a Reverse Mortgage as
a universal puzzle piece for financial planning. Why
is it a *universal* piece? Because of its adaptability to
be integrated into both simple and complex financial
plans. A Reverse Mortgage has the potential to meet
the current needs and future goals of the borrower.
Each borrower's financial picture will ultimately look
a bit different from another's. One person may need

a stable income to make the budget work—*she could use a tenure payment*. Another couple may be doing just fine right now in terms of health and income, but they want extra security in case of an unexpected event—*they would benefit from setting up a line of credit*. Grandparents may find themselves raising grandchildren—*a lump-sum payment to pay off an existing mortgage will free up monthly cash flow to accommodate this new responsibility*. Every situation is unique, and a Reverse Mortgage can be used to fit any number of scenarios.

The following are stories of how some borrowers have used these universal puzzle pieces to *complete*, *enhance*, or in some cases, *save* their financial plan. In each example, the numbers used are the ones associated with transactions occurring between 2011 and 2021. Home prices have changed dramatically over that time, and in some instances, Reverse Mortgage guidelines and pricing have changed, but the concepts behind the numbers have not. The idea is to see the possibilities a Reverse Mortgage may hold for homeowners in various situations.

INCREASING INCOME

Note: I am not a Medicaid expert. No one in my company is a Medicaid expert. We defer to the experts when it comes to structuring a loan for someone receiving Medicaid because we do not want the loan to be the reason they lose their benefits.

This borrower was sixty-four years old, on Medicaid, receiving Social Security payments, and living in his home with no mortgage.

When all was said and done, his Reverse Mortgage more than doubled his monthly income while keeping his income below the Medicaid eligibility threshold. Here is what it looked like:

Owned a home, free and clear, appraised at $322,000.

Social Security income	$849/month
Reverse Mortgage monthly income (tenure payment)	$890/month
New monthly income	$1,739/month

Regardless of income level, the opportunity to double that income will be life-changing. One big caveat to this scenario is that the borrower is an adult human being who has both the right and the ability to make his own decisions. Reverse Mortgage payments can be changed by the borrower. This loan was originally structured to provide the borrower with guaranteed monthly income without jeopardizing his Medicaid benefit status. If he should wake up one morning and decide he wants to take out a lump sum of mad money and hit the town, he has every right to do so . . . and he bears all the responsibility for that decision. It will not be the fault of the Reverse Mortgage, the lender, or the loan originator if he loses his Medicaid benefits by changing how he receives the loan proceeds. This loan was set up in such a way as to keep the borrower on the Medicaid compliance "straight and narrow," but loan originators do not monitor loans, and lenders only expect borrowers to stay in compliance with the terms of the loan contract. Lenders are not concerned about whether or not borrowers comply with Medicaid rules.

STAY HOME OR MOVE TO
SUBSIDIZED HOUSING?

It is not uncommon for a senior who has recently lost a life partner to sell a home before counting
all the costs. Sometimes this is a knee-jerk reaction
by adult children—"Dad is gone, so Mom should sell
the house," but they do not have a plan for where
Mom should live and think they will work out those
details as the situation unfolds. Other times, it is a
recently widowed senior who takes a cursory look at
the new state of the finances and determines there
is no way to stay in the home. This borrower story should encourage everyone to stop, take a deep
breath, and fully analyze the financial situation before making any rash decisions.

This borrower was a recently widowed woman
who realized that her fixed income would not cover
her mortgage payment and other monthly expenses after her husband passed away. When her husband was alive, they were financially comfortable
and able to meet all their obligations with two Social

Security checks. Fortunately, before she put a for-sale sign in the yard, a family member encouraged her to determine if there was an alternative to selling her home. She had just over 50 percent equity in her home. With a Reverse Mortgage refinance, she eliminated the mortgage payment and was able to stay in her home at a lower monthly cost than if she had sold the house, dissipated her assets, applied for, and been granted subsidized housing.

A quick explanation here on "maintenance costs." This is a government calculation of $0.14 per square foot to estimate utilities and basic upkeep costs. Of course, reality may vary from borrower to borrower and home to home, but this is the basis of the calculations noted in this book.

Here is the breakdown of the borrower's situation:

Owned a home worth $283,000 with a $123,752 mortgage.

Taxes, insurance, and maintenance costs with a Reverse Mortgage	$364/month
Estimated subsidized housing costs based on 30 percent of her fixed income	$537/month

Ultimately, the question came down to where she would rather live. The choice was between remaining in the home she shared with her husband for many years or selling, renting, exhausting the proceeds of sale, and applying to a subsidized senior housing development. She decided to use a Reverse Mortgage to stay in her home.

TO DOWNSIZE OR NOT TO DOWNSIZE?

That is the question, isn't it? Whether you call it downsizing or rightsizing, the concept, at face value, makes a lot of sense. The kids are out of the house, the house feels too large and empty, and the chore of maintaining the yard and the house becomes harder and harder as joints stiffen and muscles do not have the same *oomph* behind them that they used to. But, if one digs a bit deeper, downsizing does not always make so much sense financially.

In this case, a couple was considering downsizing their home to save money each month. The plan was to sell their home and then purchase a condo with cash, resulting in no more mortgage payments. Makes sense, right? Let's take a look at the numbers:

Owned a home worth $440,000 with a $223,676 mortgage.

Taxes, insurance, and maintenance costs with a Reverse Mortgage	$700/ month
Taxes, insurance, HOA, and maintenance costs on a free-and-clear condo	$737/ month

Since the primary purpose in considering a move was to save money, this couple decided to stay in their existing home with a Reverse Mortgage. There are service providers who can help with the maintenance and upkeep of a home. It is not difficult to find either an ambitious teenager to help with yard work or hire a professional landscaper.

If a move is being considered primarily to be in another town or to live closer to family and the decision is made to downsize simultaneously, that makes sense. However, if the purpose is solely to save money and a complete list of moving expenses has not been made and properly compared to staying at home with a Reverse Mortgage, it is possible to end up in a downsized, but more expensive, living situation. In addition, selling an existing home without a destination in mind may result in the money from the sale disappearing much faster than anticipated in the form of rent. Depending on the housing market, so much money may go to rent while waiting for the right place to become available that once it does, it is no longer affordable. This is not meant to encourage or discourage a move. The key point is to encourage homeowners to consider all the costs before selling their homes.

FUNDS FOR IN-HOME PRIVATE-PAY CARE

Family members initiated the next two stories, and the loans were each handled by a POA or Power of Attorney. When a homeowner reaches a point where she cannot manage her care, her family has some decisions to make. They can either liquidate assets to pay for her care, the children can provide or pay for care, the homeowner can spend down to Medicaid, or she can get a Reverse Mortgage. Combinations of these options and others are available as well, but these are the most common.

The idea of selling off assets is certainly a valid one. The biggest concern will be if the homeowner is heading toward Medicaid because any sales of assets for less than market value may impact her Medicaid look-back period.

As for the children stepping in, this option can solve many problems and cause quite a few. If adult children stop working to care for an elder, they lose income and may tap into their Social Security payments sooner than is advisable. Depending on *where* care is provided, in the adult child's home or the elder's home, the adult child may find herself, upon the death of her care recipient, in a home she does not own and without enough recent job history to afford to refinance the home into her name or find alternate housing for herself.

If adult children opt to pay for their loved one's care rather than provide the care themselves, they should take a serious look at what that cost may entail—not just in the moment but into the future. Children may be quick to pay for care, believing they will recover the cost when the parent's home sells, but if the parent ends up on Medicaid, a Medicaid estate recovery claim could mean the equity from the home goes to Medicaid instead of the children.

Using Medicaid to finance long-term care is an option, but if the person needing assistance must move to community care without any funds for a Medicaid spend down, her choices for *where* to receive care will be severely limited. The purpose of mentioning these alternatives is not to advocate one over another but to encourage all parties—parents and adult children—to become educated concerning Medicaid rules long before the need arises.

This brings us, of course, to the option of using a Reverse Mortgage to tap into an elder's home value to, essentially, use her home to keep her in her home. Here are two examples:

A ninety-nine-year-old man had a free-and-clear home worth $110,000. He was able to access $79,000 as a line of credit. These funds helped to replace the furnace in his home and pay for private-pay in-home care.

In his case, the gentleman's seventy-five-year-old niece was overseeing his affairs. She signed the loan on his behalf as his Power of Attorney and was able to keep him in the home where he wanted to be longer than would have been possible without the Reverse Mortgage.

A 104-year-old woman had a free-and-clear home worth $265,000. Her Reverse Mortgage provided a $190,000 line of cred-

it drawn upon to help pay for 24/7 in-home care for the rest of her life.

Admittedly, people question the motives behind originating a loan for a 104-year-old. In fact, the family considered referrals for placement and community care *instead* of going through the loan process. However, in this case, a granddaughter was the driving force behind this loan, and all four of our borrower's octogenarian children fully supported the loan. This was a family decision that resulted in a woman staying in the home she loved, the home she and her husband bought together and where they raised their family until the end of her days. As with the previous example, a family member, who was the borrower's Power of Attorney, signed this loan.

THE BEST TIME TO GET A REVERSE MORTGAGE

This is what everyone wants to know. *When* is the most strategic time to get a Reverse Mortgage?

Since older age means access to more of the home value, is it better to wait? Is it smarter to deplete other assets before considering a Reverse Mortgage? Surely you should only explore a Reverse Mortgage when there are no other options, right? Most eligible homeowners who hear the words "Reverse Mortgage" respond with, "*I have paid off my mortgage! Why in the world would I want another one? I'm never going to have another mortgage as long as I live!*"

The thing is, *the best time to get a Reverse Mortgage is when you don't need one.* Yes, you read that right. The best time to get a Reverse Mortgage is when you don't need one. Think of it as insurance. Insurance is one thing we all buy and hope we never need. The best time to get a Reverse Mortgage is when the borrower is in good health, probably still working, and there is no crisis looming on the horizon. Why? It is difficult, although not impossible, for a borrower to go through the process of getting a Reverse Mortgage when she is already in crisis—financially, medically, or emotionally. For some borrowers, the process of locating paperwork and preparing for an appraisal can be stressful under the best of circumstances. If the borrower is already at risk of losing her home, is recovering from a health scare, or has recently lost her life partner, these tasks can feel even more daunting.

Unfortunately, very few people, particularly those who have sworn off mortgages forever—*no ifs, ands, or buts*—will consider the idea of planning in such a manner. Even among individuals who believe a Reverse Mortgage is a good option for them, many think this is something they can take care of later or give more thought to in the future, should a need arise. *In the moments of sunshine and blue skies, it can be easy to forget what it feels like to be threatened by an unexpected storm of circumstances.* How often do we hear someone say, "I never thought something like this would happen to me"? It is necessary to find a balance between living in a world of gloom and doom, expecting the worst, and living in a world of denial with no rainy-day preparations.

Fortunately, some borrowers are more proactive about planning for their future and have learned through life experiences not to take anything for granted. One such case was a woman who had worked in the healthcare industry. She fully understood and had seen in her patients how quickly life could change. She sought out a Reverse Mortgage because she wanted to make sure that she would be in the best possible financial situation to deal with an unexpected crisis. She did not need the money when her loan was originated, and she knew that if she did not tap into her line of credit, it would grow over time, building upon itself and helping to protect her future.

When her loan was originated in 2015, she started with a line of credit worth about $193,000. Looking at her estimated amortization schedule and the expected interest rates at the time of her loan, if she did not touch the funds, she could have had over $252,000 available to her in 2020. Bear in mind, loan originators have no way of knowing if a borrower has accessed any of her funds. This simply demonstrates the growth potential for an untouched Reverse Mortgage line of credit.

REDUCED PRESSURE TO CONTINUE WORKING

A recent conversation with a seventy-six-year-old gentleman illustrates how powerful a preemptive Reverse Mortgage could be. He has been a recruiter for the past thirty-five years, and when COVID struck, his business disappeared for all practical purposes. Companies were laying off employees, others were closing altogether, and many of his clients were not hiring because of worldwide economic uncertainty. As was the case for many people, he had not financially prepared for 2020. While he has not closed a deal in over a year, his business could pick right back up as the economy reopens. If this gentleman already had a Reverse Mortgage in place, he would not have needed to worry about making a mortgage payment while he had no income. He could have been paying down his Reverse Mortgage loan balance during the months when business was booming, but then when business slowed down, he could have stopped making those optional payments. Think of the emotional stress this could have alleviated through 2020. Rather than worrying about making ends meet throughout the year, he could have focused on how his business could pivot to serve the changing employment landscape during COVID and beyond.

CREATIVE USE OF LOAN PROCEEDS

This borrower story is a prime example of how to use a Reverse Mortgage for income potential. A borrower owned her own mortgage-free home when she inherited another house that had an existing mortgage. She decided to take out a Reverse Mortgage on her primary residence and use the proceeds to pay off the mortgage on the house she inherited. She now owns two houses with no monthly mortgage payments due on either one. She lives in the house with the Reverse Mortgage and rents out the other. She still must pay taxes, insurance, any HOA fees, and maintenance on both houses, but the income from the rental more than covers the costs of both. In addition, she decided to make payments to her Reverse Mortgage balance equal to the interest and monthly mortgage insurance to keep the balance from rising. As a result, she will have access to a larger line of credit, or higher tenure payments, if she needs the money later.

Imagine having an untapped Reverse Mortgage line of credit set up and steadily growing. One day, you happen across the perfect place for a vacation home or an investment property. Instead of needing to go through the mortgage process while hoping no one else closes the deal first, the freedom associated with a line of credit might allow the flexibility to make a cash offer and have the deal closed before anyone else has even figured out the next step. This is both the opportunity *and the hazard* of a line of credit. Some people cannot stand to have money available and not spend it!

BRINGING FLEXIBILITY
TO A WHOLE NEW LEVEL

Here are the details of the borrower mentioned in the introduction of this book. It is a powerful example of how to take advantage of the flexibility

available through a Reverse Mortgage. This borrower was not necessarily resistant to the idea of
a Reverse Mortgage but was one of those individuals who considered it to be a *good* idea, not an
urgent idea. The urgency changed when, at the
age of eighty-two, she lost her job. While working, she met her monthly financial obligations, including mortgage and credit card payments. Once
she found herself relying strictly on Social Security income, the situation was drastically different.
Thankfully, she reached out quickly after losing
her job and did not allow herself to get into a situation she could not get out of without losing her
house.

*Home value of $550,000 with a monthly mort-
gage payment of $665.74.*

A Reverse Mortgage provided her with:

Lump-sum payment to pay off existing mortgage	$70,800
Cash out to pay off credit card debt and make home repairs	$60,000
Tenure payment from the remaining Principal Limit after the lump-sum payments	$1,455/ month
Paying off her existing mortgage and credit card debt	$2,325/ month
Total monthly cash flow change	$3,780/ month

Imagine the difference this is going to make in her life for years to come. If she decides to look for work again, it will be because she wants to, not because she has to.

REFINANCING A REVERSE MORTGAGE

As with a traditional forward mortgage, a Reverse Mortgage can be refinanced. When a borrower mentions an existing Reverse Mortgage, it is important to determine if refinancing would be in her best interest. Of particular concern is if home values in the area have appreciated since the Reverse Mortgage was originated. The next two examples demonstrate the value of considering a Reverse Mortgage refinance. (Please note: "LOC" is the acronym for line of credit.)

Refinance Example #1:

Remaining balance on Reverse Mortgage LOC from 2013	$24,625
New Reverse Mortgage in 2017	$5,000 cash out $43,310 LOC

Refinance Example #2:

Remaining balance on Reverse Mortgage LOC from 2006	$15,675
New Reverse Mortgage LOC in 2016	$114,424

In the first example, there was enough home value increase in only four years to justify a refinance. The second example is more extreme because a decade had passed since the first Reverse Mortgage was originated. There is a requirement that an FHA Reverse Mortgage cannot be refinanced to another FHA Reverse Mortgage for at least eighteen months. All borrowers, no matter what type of loan is in place, should make a habit of an Annual Mortgage Review. This provides the homeowner with a home value update, information about whether interest rates have shifted in their favor, and an evaluation to determine if any changes in their marital status, family size, employment, etc., may indicate a benefit from refinancing their loan. Much like reviewing legal documents and insurance coverage, an annual review can either prompt a change or provide peace of mind. There is a lot to be said for knowing you are in the best possible mortgage for your unique circumstances.

CO-BORROWERS

Speaking of changing and unique circumstances, this example demonstrates how changing a mortgage can meet the changing needs of borrowers. A real estate agent referred a couple to us for a Reverse Mortgage due to the husband's poor health. The concern was that if they sold their home, there was not a realistic option to purchase another that would meet their needs and lower their expenses. At the time, they owed too much on their home to qualify for a Reverse Mortgage, so they refinanced with a traditional mortgage to lower their payments and preserve as much equity as possible.

Within three years, the property had appreciated enough to qualify for a refinance into a Reverse Mortgage. The husband's health continued to deteriorate, and this loan allowed them to stay in their home with a son providing live-in care for his father. Two years later, the husband had passed away, and the live-in son was now over sixty-two. They decided to refinance the Reverse Mortgage with the mother and son as co-borrowers. The son can now remain in the home to help his mother but will not have his living situation jeopardized when his mother is no longer living in the home. It is not uncommon for live-in caregiving adult children to find themselves with nowhere to live when their parent passes away and a mortgage comes due. Often the adult child finds himself living in a home he does not own and, due to the demands of caring for an elderly parent, without any recent outside income. By wisely using the advantages of a Reverse Mortgage, the borrowers in this example have effectively planned to mitigate a future housing crisis for the caregiving son.

ARE YOU A PLANNER?

Several years ago, a past borrower decided he wanted to live in his old neighborhood again. At the time, he was in his late fifties and was on a fixed income, including a disability payment that would cease when he turned sixty-five. After analyzing his situation and goals, he concluded that he could purchase the home he desired with a traditional loan right away. If he would be diligent with payments, and based on anticipated growth in home values, he should be able to refinance to a Reverse Mortgage between the age of eligibility at sixty-two and the time his income would drop at age sixty-five. This would enable him to remain in his home, with no future mortgage payments, even when his income decreased. Scenarios like this demonstrate the advantage of working with a loan originator who will take the time to understand each client and who is willing to look beyond an immediate transaction. Rather than viewing each piece in isolation, it must be determined how all the pieces can fit together to complement each other and form a complete financial picture.

ASSETS, BUT SHORT ON CASH

This borrower had substantial assets but was short on cash. After hearing a Reverse Mortgage presentation, his daughter encouraged him to explore this option. He owned his home free and clear, had a storage unit business, and two additional rental properties. He lived comfortably on his rental income and Social Security payments, but his properties had deferred maintenance. As a retired contractor, he knew that he could either increase the rent or sell his properties at a higher price if he took care of some upgrades. A Reverse Mortgage provided him with $100,000 cash at closing and additional funds available in a line of credit, giving him the cash he needed to upgrade his properties.

JUST IN CASE

A financial planner referred this couple. With minimal savings and no investments, they were not *working* with the financial planner, but he recognized the potential for serious problems down the road and wanted to help them make some changes before they were in an unfixable situation. They had the option of a traditional mortgage or a Reverse Mortgage. They liked the lower closing costs and low rate available with a traditional mortgage, but understood that two incomes were necessary to make the required payments. If either spouse died, the survivor would not be able to remain in the home. A Reverse Mortgage gave them the option to start a savings plan by making payments against the loan balance as if it were a traditional loan. They also had peace of mind, knowing that if their income decreased or if either spouse passed away, the other could remain in the home.

COMBINING HOUSEHOLDS

A tax preparer referred a recently married couple working to combine their households. Both were still employed, and each owned a home. Rather than move into either of their current homes, they planned to purchase a home together and then retire. After selling one home, they used the cash from the sale and their combined incomes to qualify for a traditional mortgage to purchase their dream home. The sale of the first home did not provide

enough cash to qualify them to make their purchase with a Reverse Mortgage, but once they
sold the second house, they could take the proceeds of that sale and refinance their new home
with a Reverse Mortgage. They are now settled
into their dream home, have no monthly mortgage
payments, and the path to retirement has been
cleared.

DECREASING STRESS

A real estate agent referred his brother and sis-
ter-in-law for a Reverse Mortgage, hoping to help
ease their stress due to his brother's deteriorating
health. The couple wanted to stay in their ranch-
style home but needed to eliminate their monthly
mortgage payment. Their Reverse Mortgage not
only eliminated that monthly payment but provided them nearly $30,000 cash at closing and about
$100,000 in a line of credit available after the first
year. This radical change in their financial situation
succeeded in reducing stress while keeping them in
their home.

COMPLETE 180

A single gentleman had been faithfully making payments on his first and second mortgages until, at age seventy-one, he realized he would never pay off his home completely. A friend suggested he explore the possibility of a Reverse Mortgage refinance. His Reverse Mortgage eliminated his monthly mortgage payments, provided $8,000 at closing as well as a $124,000 line of credit. This complete turnaround from his house *draining* his assets to his house *providing* cash flow made his retirement far more comfortable.

UNEXPECTED BENEFIT DURING A CRISIS

A friend referred a sixty-nine-year-old widow who was still working and making mortgage payments. Her Reverse Mortgage refinance eliminated her monthly mortgage payments and provided her with a $5,000 line of credit. She called several months later, thrilled to have had her mortgage payments eliminated because, during the height of the

COVID crisis, she was able to stop working her retail job without worrying about losing her home. She was confident in her ability to wait out the crisis and plans to return to work when she feels safe to do so.

PLANNING FOR A MEDICAID SPEND DOWN

A sixty-six-year-old gentleman was living independently but required a conservator to manage his financial affairs. His attorney and his conservator were concerned about the rapid depletion of his assets. His Reverse Mortgage eliminated his monthly mortgage payment, provided about $25,000 cash at closing, and a $90,000 line of credit available after one year. This refinance allowed him to stay in his home while leaving more than $250,000 in equity for a Medicaid spend down when he can no longer live independently.

UNPLANNED RETIREMENT

This couple was encouraged to consider a Reverse Mortgage by their daughter. Both the husband

and wife were sixty-seven, and they had serious financial concerns on the horizon. Due to residual health issues after a car accident, the husband knew his ability to remain employed at his physical job was coming to an end. The wife was not working outside of the home, so they were dependent on his income. By refinancing to a Reverse Mortgage, they eliminated their monthly mortgage payment and now have a guaranteed monthly tenure payment of nearly $670 for as long as they live in the home and comply with other loan terms. These two factors resulted in a nearly $1,800 positive cash flow change to their monthly budget.

3 | THE LOAN PROCESS

With a better understanding of the basics of a Reverse Mortgage, who qualifies, and the flexibility they offer, now is a good time to explore the process of obtaining a Reverse Mortgage. There are some differences between this loan product and conventional loan products that should be explained.

The loan process typically starts by talking to a loan originator. In our practice, we will prepare a proposal package with preliminary numbers for at least three loan/pricing scenarios. The focus will be on what the borrower hopes to accomplish and if there is enough equity to reach the borrower's goal. The only personal information required to provide an estimate includes 1) the birthdate of the borrower, 2) the property address, and 3) the outstanding balance of any loans or liens currently against the property. At this stage, loan scenarios can be based on either the borrower's home value estimate or one from another source such as Zillow.

This discussion should explore options that the borrower can currently qualify for and options she may qualify for later. It may be beneficial to wait for the home to appreciate before starting the process in cases where there is not enough equity. There could be delinquent taxes that must be made current before proceeding. An unmarried couple with one partner over sixty-two and the other under sixty-two should decide if they want to proceed with a Reverse Mortgage in only the older partner's name, if they want to marry and originate the loan with the younger as a Qualified Non-Borrowing Spouse, or wait until the younger partner is sixty-two so that both will be qualified borrowers on the loan. Sometimes the choices are easy, and sometimes they are more complicated. Varying state laws can affect these options.

COUNSELING

Included in a loan proposal package is a list of FHA-approved counselors and a description of the mandatory counseling process. (The Federal Housing Administration or FHA is part of HUD, the US Department of Housing and Urban Development). *The purpose of counseling is to verify that the borrower understands the loan product, her obligations as a borrower, and the fact that taking out this loan will impact the amount of equity available when she, or her heirs, choose to sell.* Borrowers are encouraged to bring an adult child or another trusted friend/advisor to counseling so more ears are hearing the same information and a higher likelihood of all interested parties understanding the process. It is advisable to have the person designated to handle your affairs when you are no longer able to in attendance at the counseling session. The borrower can choose any counselor on the list, and a loan originator may not steer or encourage the borrower to use a particular counselor. Counseling takes about an hour and can be done over the phone, by virtual conference, or in person. Some counselors charge for this service, and others provide it at no cost to the borrower because of their organization's funding. There are often waitlists for the no-cost options, but a motivated borrower who is eager to get her loan process started can usually get a fee-based appointment within a day or two.

DOCUMENTATION

Once counseling has been completed and the loan originator receives a signed copy of the counseling certificate, information for a complete loan application may be collected online, over the phone, or in person. A borrower will have to provide documentation to prove her eligibility to qualify based on income, assets, and credit. She will also have to show that her taxes, insurance, and any HOA dues have been paid on time and in full for at least the previous twenty-four months if she does not want a Life Expectancy Set Aside. Depending upon the borrower's circumstances, required documentation will include what is typical for any full documentation loan such as pay stubs, pension or Social Security award letters, tax returns, and bank statements.

APPRAISAL

Every FHA Reverse Mortgage requires an FHA appraisal. An FHA appraisal determines the value of the home for loan purposes and evaluates the property for health and safety concerns. Common concerns discovered during the FHA appraisal process include broken windows, missing handrails, peeling paint on homes built before 1978, roof defects, etc. Depending on the issue, it may have to be corrected before closing, or a repair set-aside may be arranged to have the repairs completed after closing. Under Appraiser Independence Rules, neither the loan originator nor the borrower may choose or influence the appraiser. Once the appraisal report is received by the loan originator, it is submitted to FHA, and they will determine if a second appraisal is necessary. If so, FHA will require the use of the lower of the two values. Appraisal costs vary greatly, depending on geography, property type, and market demand, but the borrower should anticipate this cost during the loan process. Her loan originator will be able to provide an estimate of this cost.

WHO WILL HANDLE YOUR AFFAIRS?

Reverse Mortgage borrowers can easily range in age from 62 to 105 years old, some of whom are still working and quite capable, while others are dealing with vision issues, hearing loss, early stages of dementia, or other challenges. Some borrowers can sign all the paperwork and provide supporting documentation, while others may request a phone call, virtual conference, or in-person meeting for additional guidance through the process. It is not unusual to work with a recently widowed individual whose spouse had handled the finances for decades. These surviving spouses are sometimes unprepared to deal with the financial issues thrust upon them and may require an extra measure of patience and guidance. However, the fact that a person needs extra help does not mean they should leave their long-time home. In many cases, a Reverse Mortgage is exactly the solution to help her stay where she wants to live.

A Reverse Mortgage is inherently designed for someone's last home. There are no restrictions on a borrower's ability to sell a home with a Reverse Mortgage, pay off the loan, and move, but generally speaking, it is a valid assumption. Most Reverse Mortgage borrowers intend to stay in their home for as long as possible, which means many may contend with reduced capacity while living in the home. A borrower may eventually no longer manage her affairs well, including paying taxes, insurance, and maintaining her home—the basic conditions of a Reverse Mortgage. The obvious question is, *"Who will handle these affairs when the borrower cannot?"*

Consulting an attorney to ensure the appropriate documents (will/trust, Power of Attorney, etc.) are in place is strongly recommended. In addition, the named person on these legal documents should know the location of a borrower's recent Reverse

Mortgage statement. These statements are issued monthly and contain crucial loan information, including contact information for the loan servicer and the loan's current balance, which is vital to the decision-making process when evaluating the pros and cons of selling, refinancing, or walking away from a property. The actual loan amount can vary greatly from the amount reflected in the public record. The dollar figure recorded with the county will be 150 percent of the property value when the loan was originated, not the amount owed.

4 REVERSE MORTGAGES AND SENIOR SERVICES

The senior service industry provides countless care and support options for seniors and their families. From hands-on caregivers to community administrators to business owners, these professionals strive to assist seniors to live in dignity and safety while honoring their choices and staying within their budgets. Still, even throughout an industry focused on providing seniors with goods and services, there can be resistance to even *hearing* the phrase "Reverse Mortgage." Much of this resistance is due to a basic misunderstanding of the utilization of Reverse Mortgages and a lack of time to seek out the facts. These service providers must understand how a Reverse Mortgage can provide opportunities for their clients to enhance their financial situation, pay for services, and maintain independence.

Reverse Mortgages provide a solution that can help numerous seniors stay in their own homes and pay for many useful services. These seniors need trusted, educated, and resourceful professionals to help them analyze all of their options and guide them along the path that is in their best interest. For some seniors, it will be in their best interest to remain in their home with a Reverse Mortgage. For others, this will not be the best solution. The key is to objectively look at all of the options and determine the best course of action.

The good news is that people are living longer, sometimes much longer than their parents. The bad news is that people are often outliving their money. It is necessary to find creative ways to stretch financial resources across more years than in previous generations.

NONPROFITS AND GOVERNMENT AGENCIES

Public assistance and grant-funded organizations are necessary services and provide crucial support for many people. However, it would be beneficial to encourage senior homeowners who are struggling financially to explore the viability of a Reverse Mortgage before enrolling them in programs that are functioning on tight budgets themselves. Think of the positive impact proper Reverse Mortgage education and utilization could have on expanding the reach of these organizations!

Grant and taxpayer-funded service providers would have the opportunity to help so many more people if first, they educate those who have the option of using a self-supporting resource (their house) and second, use the dollars that would have been dispensed to these borrowers for the people who don't own their own home, can't meet their own needs, or don't have anywhere else to turn but to public assistance programs.

This is by no means a strike against these entities but rather a suggestion on using funds most effectively. The challenge is to implement effective methods of getting education into the minds and information into the hands of the right people early enough to have a meaningful impact. If the suggestion to consider a Reverse Mortgage is not provided early enough in the vortex of a downward financial spiral, the opportunity may be lost. Far too often, a senior homeowner will sell her home due to a lack of other known options, pay rent, and run out of money. She may have been better served by remaining in her home with a Reverse Mortgage.

Providing basic subject matter to social work students, in-house continuing education programs to employees, and scheduling ongoing informational seminars for clients are suggestions for enhancing the approach to this topic within government and nonprofit organizations.

COMMUNITY-BASED CARE PROVIDERS

At first glance, it may appear that a Reverse Mortgage loan originator and the leasing or marketing manager for a care community are working against each other. The loan originator offers a solution to help a senior stay in her home, and the leasing manager offers a solution for community living. However, this does not have to be considered a conflict. Reverse Mortgages, as versatile as they are, are not the answer for every senior. Likewise, community-based care is not the answer for every senior. If the focus of both professionals is the best interest of the senior, both should be knowledgeable about the alternatives available if their services are not the right fit.

Going back to the story of the loan provided to the 104-year-old woman, her family was offered referrals to placement agencies before the loan application process began. The family felt keeping her in her home was the better option.

It would be advantageous for community care providers to share basic information about Reverse

Mortgages as a viable option for seniors and their families who take a tour and determine community care is not currently the right solution for them. However, what if community care *is* the right fit for someone, but there's a waiting list? COVID certainly put a strain on communities, and there are not the same sort of waitlists now that there were before, but it is only a matter of time before occupancy rates are on the rise and waiting lists are once again a factor in senior housing. Providing a Reverse Mortgage solution while a future resident is on a waiting list may help keep her from looking for a community *without* a waiting list and help her financially in the meantime. This is particularly important if the senior requires either additional care or adaptive living solutions that funds from a Reverse Mortgage could help finance. Knowing that a future resident is as safe as possible in her home environment means she is likely to still be a candidate for moving in when her turn comes up on the waitlist.

Finally, and particularly for communities that provide memory care or skilled nursing, it is not uncommon for one person in a couple to need commu-

nity-based care while the other is able to, and de-
sirous of, staying home. In this situation, a Reverse
Mortgage may help provide spend-down assistance
or private-pay care for one spouse while securing
the couple's home for the other. This is a situation
where having a Reverse Mortgage in place sooner
rather than later is certainly important and should
be part of the conversation early on when families
explore their options for future care.

PLACEMENT SERVICES
AND REAL ESTATE AGENTS

As with the explanation provided for communi-
ty-care settings, placement agents who realize that
either the type of community a family is seeking is
not financially viable or that someone is considering placement for reasons that could be addressed
more cost-effectively with adaptations to the home
or alternate types of care providers, it is all about
understanding the resources available. Will placement agents be paid a commission to refer clients to
a loan originator instead of helping them move into

a community? No. Not only might clients question a professional's motives, but the mortgage industry does not allow for kickbacks. Once again, it is about doing the right thing for each client and knowing that in the long run, a good reputation is more important, and more valuable, than the next sale.

A placement agent referred a woman with early-stage dementia for a Reverse Mortgage. She was still living in her own home, and both she and her family wanted to explore her options. Her disease had not progressed to a point where community-based memory care was necessary for her safety. They decided together on a Reverse Mortgage because it served two purposes: First, it allowed her to remain in her home while she was safe to be there. Second, it made cash available to pay for the first months of care when it is time for her to move. A year and a half later, money from her line of credit was used to pay for her first months of care in a memory care community. This made it possible for an orderly transition to community care and the sale of her home to pay for ongoing care. The professional who referred her did not *give up* a placement but rather *delayed* the placement so the client could remain in her home longer and then transition to a community at the appropriate time. This professional also gained another placement from the same family.

This same concept applies to real estate agents who determine that a move is not in a client's best interest. Recommending a way for a client to stay in her current home does not necessarily mean the real estate agent has lost a client, but rather a delayed sale met the best interests of a client. *It is a powerful recommendation for a client to talk about a real estate agent who showed her the options rather than encouraged her to sell when there were no desirable alternatives for her next home.* This professional is not just in business to close the next deal at any cost but rather cares about clients and reputation.

PRIVATE-PAY SERVICES

Whether a company provides in-home care, meal preparation, cleaning and maintenance, care management, private transportation, or any other service that helps seniors stay in their homes safer and more comfortably, basic knowledge about Reverse Mortgages is imperative. Why? *Because these loans are a funding source for private-pay services.*

It is not unusual to speak with business owners who have had clients cut back on services for strictly financial reasons. Those same clients are often unwilling to consider a Reverse Mortgage because of negative stories about these loans. A client might welcome the extra help but feels her budget cannot accommodate the funds to pay for the services . . . even though her home is mortgage-free and worth hundreds of thousands of dollars! There is a high likelihood that a client in this situation will experience a fall, not care for herself properly, or her home will fall into disrepair if she does not have assistance. However, because of misunderstandings about Reverse Mortgages, she will not even consider one as an option to pay for services. The most common misconception here is that if she gets a Reverse Mortgage, she will not have anything left to leave for her children as an inheritance. *Many* adult children would rather have their parents in a safe environment, with the assistance they need, than inherit an empty house.

In some cases, rather than support the idea of a Reverse Mortgage, the senior's adult children pay for her care out of their own pockets, expecting to recover these expenses when they inherit the house. It is often overlooked that if the parent eventually ends up on Medicaid (and many do), Medicaid's estate recovery process has the first claim to any assets that might have otherwise been part of the children's inheritance. In cases like this, it might be better if the parent's care is paid through Reverse Mortgage proceeds rather than out of the children's resources since they may not receive reimbursement through an inheritance. This is not a one-size-fits-all situation, so it is always advisable to consider the larger financial implications for everyone involved.

The idea here is not to have a service provider's staff encourage every client to get a Reverse Mortgage, but rather to encourage those seniors and their family members to explore their options. A conversation with a Reverse Mortgage loan originator can answer questions, alleviate concerns, and provide guidance to fully explore the options. Family members should be encouraged to meet with the loan originator, and service providers may consider being part of the initial conversation. They have built a relationship of trust with the client, and she may need guidance to find a trustworthy Reverse Mortgage professional.

INSURANCE-BASED SERVICES

It makes sense that private-pay service providers want to be aware of Reverse Mortgages as a funding source for their services, but what about service providers paid through insurance? Whether an organization provides nursing care, therapies, hospice, case management, or any other insurance-paid service, it is in a client's best interest for her providers to be as well-versed as possible about any products and services that can enhance her life, decrease her stress, and increase her sense of financial and housing security. Depending on the type of service and the payor arrangement for insurance-based services, time with a client is limited—both per visit and number of visits. When time with a client is coming to an end and she would benefit from additional care provided on a private-pay basis, most professionals will make those recommendations. Consider how much more impactful— *and apt to be followed*—those recommendations will be if clients are given options for paying for those additional services. Regularly providing information on how to pay for home modifications and other private-pay services may also decrease hospital readmission rates. Having been involved in a client's life during or immediately following a health crisis, there is trust in this relationship, and any recommendations will be taken seriously. As with the suggestion that private-pay service providers assist their client in connecting with a reputable loan originator, that same approach holds true here. Guide her to an expert in the field who can help her navigate her options and evaluate them objectively.

FINANCIAL SERVICES

Financial planners, advisors, wealth managers, and investment brokers, while not all doing the same thing, are all involved in guiding individuals through the various tangles of finances with the goal of planning for and living a well-funded retirement. Previously, Reverse Mortgages were referred to as puzzle pieces because they can be used to fill various holes in a financial picture. Financial service providers should explore how a Reverse Mortgage can augment other income streams or keep clients from tapping into other resources too early, which may have tax implications or penalties.

A Reverse Mortgage could be used to provide liquidity to high-net-worth individuals who own a business or other non-liquid assets. It may be an attractive option for a person making mortgage payments with withdrawals from tax-sheltered accounts. It may eliminate the risk associated with periodic requalifying for a home equity line of credit. A Reverse Mortgage line of credit can reduce the stress of high volatility in other investments such as stocks, bonds, and mutual funds. The point is to look at a Reverse Mortgage in the context of a total financial plan instead of as a product in isolation.

WORKING TOGETHER FOR SENIORS

One last story for the professionals in the senior service industry.

A few years ago, a woman reached out seeking help for a friend. This friend was having problems affording food and needed assistance with personal care and the upkeep and management of her home. She lived in a house with no mortgage. The home value was more than the FHA maximum lendable value at the time. This meant that with a Reverse Mortgage, she could have had more than $300,000 to help with her expenses, upkeep on her home, and fund private-pay care for her personal needs.

Who knows how many senior service professionals in both the public and private sectors had been a part of this woman's journey over the years? If one, or ideally several, of them had brought up the subject of a Reverse Mortgage to help her stay in her home longer and safer, perhaps she would have at least given the idea some consideration. Sometimes people need to hear about their options from more than one source to help change their perceptions. Please consider sharing your newfound knowledge about Reverse Mortgages with clients, and perhaps by working together, we can make a positive difference in their lives!

5 CREATIVE LIVING WITH A REVERSE MORTGAGE

Reverse Mortgages are exceptional financial tools and are worth taking the time to understand for every eligible homeowner. A Reverse Mortgage will not be the best solution for everyone, but it is better to *know* this and have all the facts before casually dismissing one without all the details. Recently, Reverse Vision, the largest provider of Reverse Mortgage software, claimed, *"1.5 million older Americans who get mortgages every year could improve their financial outlook with a Reverse Mortgage.*[1] These numbers indicate that Reverse Mortgages are seriously underused. Many eligible borrowers who choose a loan product other than a Reverse Mortgage would fare better with a Reverse Mortgage.

Chapter 2 shared stories about the versatility of Reverse Mortgages and how they can be structured to a borrower's best advantage. Now it is time to explore additional creative ways to stay in a home while taking advantage of the benefits of a Reverse Mortgage. The key point here is that the *"why"* of this product has many more answers than a traditional forward mortgage. With a traditional forward mortgage, the issues reduce to just a few questions:

- Is it better to rent or buy?
- Is it possible to lower an interest rate or monthly payment?
- How much cash can be taken out for either debt consolidation or other purposes?

---

[1]   The Federal Housing Administration endorsed 44,661 Reverse Mortgage loans in 2020.

Alternatively, every borrower comes into a Reverse Mortgage from a slightly different direction and has specific goals. Balancing the budget, or better yet, tipping it in the borrower's favor, is the most obvious reason to have a meeting with a loan originator. For a borrower with the foresight, a Reverse Mortgage will be put into place before she needs it for a just-in-case scenario, like insurance. Remember, a Reverse Mortgage has the power to eliminate mandatory monthly mortgage payments, increase cash flow, or both.

At times, all a Reverse Mortgage can do in a particular case is eliminate the monthly mortgage payment. This sounds so offhand or even inconsequential, but it is not inconsequential at all! The reality of not having to make a monthly mortgage payment can have a significant positive impact. It can be the difference between staying in a beloved home or being forced to sell. It can be the difference between choosing to make a mortgage payment or buying food or medication. It can be the difference between going to work because of necessity or going to work because of desire. The list goes on and on. For a retiree on a fixed income, eliminating a sin-gle monthly bill is significant. When the eliminated bill is a mortgage payment, it can be life-changing.

But what about the other side of the budget, the *income* side? For a borrower who likes to know exactly how much money is coming in each month and wants the security of having regular guaranteed payments, a tenure payment will bring the peace of mind she needs. For the borrower who wants a fi-nancial boost for a certain amount of time and wants to control how big that boost will be, a term payment may be right for her. A borrower who will benefit from the line of credit option may already feel confident in her ability to live within her means and does not *need* the extra money right now. She is probably hoping she will never need the extra money, but she sleeps better at night knowing that if an unexpected need arises, a unique opportunity appears, or the chance to help a friend or family member presents itself, she will be able to make her decision based on whether she wants to, not affordability.

A good example is a borrower who lived in her home for forty-two years and wanted to see if she could "loosen her budget" a bit at eighty years of age. She had never been a high-wage earner but had paid off her mortgage through subsistence jobs and a frugal lifestyle. Her Reverse Mortgage provided her with $1,000 cash at closing, a $72,000 line of credit, and a guaranteed monthly tenure payment of $500 for as long as she lives in her home and complies with other loan terms.

What about the more emotional reasons behind needing to adjust one's financial situation? A prime example is when grandparents find themselves raising grandchildren. Regardless of the reason behind this multi-generational household, it will impact the grandparents' budget. A gentleman wanted to refinance his home. He was still working but wanted to lower his monthly payments to put some wiggle room in the finances because he and his wife would be raising their grandchild. Upon evaluation, he considered a Reverse Mortgage rather than the traditional refinance he had been originally seeking. Even though he was still working and could manage the monthly mortgage payments of a traditional refinance, it was more impactful to eliminate those mortgage payments.

Caring for a younger generation is certainly a possibility, but as time goes on, the potential of needing to care for someone of the same genera-tion—a life partner or a sibling—is an even strong-er possibility. Everyone knows friends or family members who have found themselves caring for a spouse. Witnessing the toll it takes—mentally, emo-tionally, physically, and financially—is profound. No one should ever presume to say that a Reverse Mortgage can solve all those concerns, but a Re-verse Mortgage *can* ease the financial burden in many cases, which in turn can ease the emotional and mental impact. A Reverse Mortgage can even lessen the *physical* demands of caregiving by pro-viding funds for hired professional help, home mod-ifications, and other practical caregiving tools. If a working caregiving spouse could step back from employment to focus on a loved one for the time they have left together, wouldn't that be important? If a partner receiving care knows that a loved one will not inherit a financial mess because of the time taken off work, wouldn't that provide comfort? It is easier to focus on the tasks at hand when finances are not a constant concern.

What are additional options for living creatively with a Reverse Mortgage? While it is impossible to have a Reverse Mortgage on a rental property that is not owner-occupied, this does not mean a homeowner could not rent space in her primary residence while also living there. For instance, a Reverse Mortgage borrower decided to rent out her extra rooms. In addition to paying rent, her tenants help with the cooking and the yard work. She has no mortgage payment, rent checks are coming in, and she has people around her to prevent isolation and help with household tasks. *These renters are essentially paying this borrower to keep her in her home.*

There is so much discord swirling around the concept of affordable housing for people of all ages. Since having housemates can bring up safety concerns, services are available to vet applicants and help match appropriate housemates. There are programs focused on connecting seniors with seniors and others that bring college students and young adults into co-housing arrangements with seniors. There are many ways for people of all ages to help one another out, not just financially but with companionship and task assistance.

Imagine an older woman living on her own in a family-size home. She does not want to leave this home but also does not need all these rooms anymore. She is concerned about being by herself if something were to go wrong. In that same town, a single mom is trying to make ends meet. She needs to have stable housing for her young family so her kids can enroll in school and she can be close to work. Apartments are expensive, and she is not yet in a financial position to purchase a house. Is there any reason that, with appropriate vetting on both sides, these two women could not help each other out? One has a house with unused rooms and is concerned about being alone. The other has a job, children and is concerned about finding affordable housing. Whether their contract is strictly monetary, an in-kind exchange of housing and childcare for chores and errands, or a combination of the two, coming together helps meet the needs of both parties and keeps them both from having to access public assistance.

The same sort of solution is possible between a college student or young professional who is trying to get herself established but is not quite there yet and an older homeowner who is, as they say, "sharp as a tack" but no longer able to maintain her home and property the way she used to. There is no reason why this young person cannot live with this older person in exchange for keeping up the property and helping to run errands. If a senior needs help with personal care or other activities of daily living (ADLs), there are opportunities for a housemate who is comfortable with and trained in caregiving to exchange care for housing. The possibilities are endless, and they not only help keep seniors in the homes they love and the neighborhoods they are familiar with, but can connect generations in an age of disconnect.

If the idea of sharing personal space by renting extra rooms is uncomfortable, there is still the ability for a Reverse Mortgage borrower to have tenants. A borrower can utilize a Reverse Mortgage on up to a four-plex. If the borrower likes the idea of rental

income but not necessarily the day-to-day responsibilities of being a landlord, she can engage the services of a property manager. The property management company gets a portion of the rental income,
but not so much that it would not make owning a du-
plex, triplex, or four-plex an attractive financial prop-
osition. Living in a home without a monthly mortgage payment that brings in rent from one to three
units is a potentially lucrative retirement option.

Another idea to consider is using a Reverse
Mortgage to *purchase* a home. Without going into
all the specifics, here is a basic summary. A qualified
buyer (sixty-two or older, purchasing a primary residence, etc.) can purchase a home with roughly 50
percent or more down and live in the home without
any monthly mortgage payments. A borrower decided that rather than *downsize*, she wanted to *upsize* in
her retirement years and purchase her dream home.
She sold her existing home and used the proceeds
as a down payment for a much pricier home. Using
a Reverse Mortgage purchase loan, she was able
to live in a home that is a significant upgrade to her
prior home, with no monthly mortgage payments.

Some might question what this does to the estate, so let's follow this transaction from the beginning to end:

June 2013: Sold her free-and-clear home for $212,900 in order to purchase a nicer home with a Reverse Mortgage.

December 2013: Purchased a $490,000 home with $241,000 cash and a Reverse Mortgage.

December 2017: Home value increased to $636,000, so refinanced her Reverse Mortgage to increase her available cash.

September 2019: Home value according to Zillow was $780,000. Shortly before her death, she sold home to person of her choice for $450,000, giving her the funds to pay off the Reverse Mortgage and them the equity in the home.

It's clear that the property value increased faster than the loan balance in this case which resulted in the equity increasing. This is why it is important for a Reverse Mortgage borrower to plan for who will get the equity. In this case, the borrower had no children or heirs, so she gave the benefit to a friend. Another option would have been to give the equity to a church or other non-profit organization.

While this book focuses on FHA Reverse Mortgages, an increasing number of non-FHA Reverse Mortgage products are available. These non-FHA products can be helpful for some borrowers. A discussion with a loan originator will help determine which product is most appropriate for a borrower's situation. Typical reasons to use a non-FHA product are to eliminate FHA mortgage insurance costs, take advantage of property values above the FHA lending limit, potentially lower closing costs, and different requirements for condominium approval and/ or appraisals. These factors should not be considered in isolation because there can be tradeoffs with many factors relating to mortgages. For example, lower closing costs may be traded for a higher interest rate, resulting in a higher line of credit growth rate. Pay attention to the draw period on a non-FHA Reverse Mortgage line of credit, as it may be shorter than with an FHA Reverse Mortgage.

CONCLUSION

Congratulations! You have learned about Reverse Mortgages, discovered how versatile they can be, and explored how to integrate them with other senior services. What I hope you take away from all of this is that Reverse Mortgages are barely scratching the surface of their potential to have a positive impact on not only the lives of the borrowers but also their families and our society at large. I would like to end this by empowering and encouraging each of you to be a voice for change.

If you are already a Reverse Mortgage borrower and you read this to reinforce your positive image of the loan product and hopefully learn something new, please share this knowledge with your friends and family. Do not forget to investigate the possibility of refinancing your Reverse Mortgage.

If you are the friend or family member of some-one who could truly benefit from a Reverse Mort-gage but is resistant because they believe in the myths surrounding this powerful tool, please share the stories, help them find a reputable loan origi-nator, and be the voice of encouragement needed before a lack of forward momentum causes them to lose their home. *Not making a decision is a decision in and of itself, and the longer someone waits to act, the fewer choices there are available.*

If you are a professional in any senior services area, continue to learn about new options and oppor-tunities for your clients. Encourage your colleagues to gain a better understanding of those choices as well. Share what you do with others and take the time to learn how their services might assist your clients. Be the professional who opens doors of possibilities and offers clients innovative solutions like Reverse Mortgages to help them achieve their goals.

As it turns out, regardless of your gender, eth-nicity, religion, finances, or political views, *denial does not prevent aging.* I am hopeful that what I have written for you here will encourage you to explore all your options and seek out the best solution to help you and the ones you love thrive for many years to come!

APPENDIX:
AMORTIZATION EXAMPLES

Potential borrowers often question why they cannot access more of the home's value at the beginning of a loan. Please note that the following two tables are for demonstration purposes only. A Reverse Mortgage loan originator can provide more accurate projections based on specific property value, closing costs, starting balance, current interest rate, borrower age, and payment amount.

TABLE A

Table A is for a sixty-two-year-old borrower with an initial loan balance of $200,000 on a home worth $500,000. The "Expected Rate" column reflects a rate of 3 percent plus 0.5 percent for FHA mortgage insurance. This rate approximates the expected rate over the life of the loan. The 0.5 percent for FHA mortgage insurance is standard for today's Reverse Mortgages. The final assumption is that the home's value will appreciate at a rate of 4 percent per year, which is also a typical assumption for current Reverse Mortgage loans.

If the interest rate over the life of the loan is about 3 percent, and the home appreciates at 4 percent, the borrower has growing equity in the home because the home value is going up faster than the loan balance.

Table A also applies if the same sixty-two-year-old borrower started with a $200,000 line of credit on a $500,000 home. In this case, the line of credit would grow at the same rate as the loan balance. If the borrower spent nothing from the line of credit, and the interest rate over the life of the loan was the expected rate of 3 percent, the borrower would have about $398,000 available at age eighty-two. Table B similarly shows how the loan balance increases with an initial draw of $1,000 and monthly payments of $1,000 to the borrower.

TABLE A

Year	Age	Rate 3%	Appreciation
		3.0% + .5%	4%
	62	$ 200,000	$ 500,000
1	63	$ 207,000	$ 520,000
2	64	$ 214,245	$ 540,800
3	65	$ 221,744	$ 562,432
4	66	$ 229,505	$ 584,929
5	67	$ 237,537	$ 608,326
6	68	$ 245,851	$ 632,660
7	69	$ 254,456	$ 657,966
8	70	$ 263,362	$ 684,285
9	71	$ 272,579	$ 711,656
10	72	$ 282,120	$ 740,122
11	73	$ 291,994	$ 769,727
12	74	$ 302,214	$ 800,516
13	75	$ 312,791	$ 832,537
14	76	$ 323,739	$ 865,838
15	77	$ 335,070	$ 900,472
16	78	$ 346,797	$ 936,491
17	79	$ 358,935	$ 973,950
18	80	$ 371,498	$ 1,012,908
19	81	$ 384,500	$ 1,053,425
20	82	$ 397,958	$ 1,095,562

TABLE B

Year	Age	Rate 3%		Appreciation
		3.0% + .5%		4%
	62	$ 1,000		$ 500,000
1	63	$ 13,193		$ 520,000
2	64	$ 25,847		$ 540,800
3	65	$ 38,944		$ 562,432
4	66	$ 52,499		$ 584,929
5	67	$ 66,529		$ 608,326
6	68	$ 81,050		$ 632,660
7	69	$ 96,080		$ 657,966
8	70	$ 111,635		$ 684,285
9	71	$ 127,735		$ 711,656
10	72	$ 144,398		$ 740,122
11	73	$ 161,644		$ 769,727
12	74	$ 179,494		$ 800,516
13	75	$ 197,969		$ 832,537
14	76	$ 217,091		$ 865,838
15	77	$ 236,881		$ 900,472
16	78	$ 257,365		$ 936,491
17	79	$ 278,565		$ 973,950
18	80	$ 300,507		$ 1,012,908
19	81	$ 323,217		$ 1,053,425
20	82	$ 346,723		$ 1,095,562

GLOSSARY AND WEB LINKS

Below are simple definitions of words throughout the book, along with web links to appropriate content.

Activities of Daily Living (ADLs): The basic skills required to take care of oneself: bathing, dressing, eating, transferring, toileting, and continence.

Amortization/Amortizing: An amortization schedule reflects an anticipated loan balance over a period of time. It will show the changes monthly or annually to reflect payments made on a traditional mortgage or the anticipated increasing balance as interest, mortgage insurance, and other fees are added to a Reverse Mortgage.

Annual Mortgage Review: The process of comparing a borrower's current mortgage with other available options to determine if a refinance would be in the borrower's best interest.

Appraiser Independence: First implemented May 1, 2009, and later included in Dodd-Frank, this prohibits loan originators from choosing or influencing an appraiser. Appraisals are ordered through an Appraisal Management Company that chooses the appraiser.

Cash for Keys: The option to turn over legal rights to the house in exchange for a sum of money rather than allow the house to go into foreclosure. This can benefit both the lender and borrower when the loan balance is greater than the home value. See Mortgagee Letter 2017-11 for details at https://www.hud.gov/sites/documents/17-11ML.PDF.

Deed of Trust: A legal document recorded at the county to tell the world the loan exists.

Eliminating a Mortgage Payment: In the context of a Reverse Mortgage, eliminating a mortgage payment means eliminating the need to make a mortgage payment to the lender each month. It does not eliminate the need to pay interest, taxes, insurance, or maintenance. A Reverse Mortgage just changes how these items are paid.

Equity: The difference between the property value and loan balance. This does not account for costs of sale if the property is to be sold.

Escrow Account: An account managed by a mortgage servicer that collects money with each mortgage payment to pay taxes and insurance when due.

Federal Housing Administration (FHA): Provides default insurance on loans made by FHA-approved lenders. https://www.hud.gov/program_offices/housing/fhahistory

FHA-Approved Counseling: Independent third-party counseling. This is a required step for every FHA Reverse Mortgage borrower to verify the loan product is understood and that the loan will be in the borrower's interest. https://www.consumerfinance.gov/find-a-housing-counselor/

FHA Reverse Mortgage Insurance: Protects both the borrower and the lender from needing to pay or absorb the difference between a high loan balance and a low home value. It also protects the borrower from a default by the lender.

Forbearance: An agreement between the lender and borrower to temporarily decrease or stop mortgage loan payments due to financial hardship. This does not eliminate the need to pay but simply delays the payments.

HECM-to-HECM Refinance: The process of refinancing an existing FHA Reverse Mortgage to a new FHA Reverse Mortgage. Generally done to access an increase in home value or add borrowers to the loan.

Home Equity Conversion Mortgage (HECM): The government name for an FHA-insured Reverse Mortgage.

Home Equity Line of Credit (HELOC): A loan available for a specified amount of time that allows the homeowners to access home equity. It is revolving credit similar to having a credit card secured by a home.

Income: In the context of loan qualification or taxes, income refers to money coming from outside sources like employment, pensions, Social Security, interest, dividends, rental income, and other similar sources. In the context of money coming from a Reverse Mortgage, "income" is considered to be the opposite of "outgo." It does not represent income as defined by income tax rules or money that can add to net worth. In a technical sense, it might better be represented as "cash flow" or "distributions from a mortgage," but for many borrowers, "income" is the common term.

Life Expectancy Set Aside (LESA): Functions like an escrow account that sets aside funds from the borrower's available line of credit or "Principal Limit" to pay property taxes and homeowner's insurance. Note that if the borrower remains in the home after the set-aside is depleted, the borrower will have to pay taxes and insurance from other sources.

Line of Credit: A portion of a Reverse Mortgage borrower's available property value that is available for her to use as needed after closing.

Lump Sum: A cash distribution from a Reverse Mortgage. These distributions are only available at closing for a fixed-rate loan. They are available at closing or as a later disbursement from the line of credit with an adjustable-rate loan.

Mandatory Obligations: FHA requires that a Reverse Mortgage be a first lien against the property. This means any existing mortgages, any other liens against the property, and closing costs must be paid at closing. If the Principal Limit of the Reverse Mortgage is less than the Mandatory Obligations, the borrower will have to bring cash to closing to make up the difference.

Maximum Lendable Value: This is the maximum home value that FHA will use for loan purposes. It is $822,375 in 2021 and is typically adjusted for inflation around January 1 of each year.

Medicaid Estate Recovery: Medicaid is the federal program that will pay for medical care when a person's money runs out. It applies to people with low income and assets, but it will allow the participant to own a home while receiving benefits. As part of the Medicaid process, Medicaid may have first rights, ahead of any heirs, to any estate assets to recover the money they have spent for care.

Medicaid Look-Back Period: A period (currently five years) before a Medicaid application that Medicaid investigates all of an applicant's financial transactions to determine if assets were transferred to others for less than fair market value.

Medicaid Spend Down: Some long-term-care communities will accept a resident that is already on Medicaid. Others are private-pay only. Between these two are communities that will accept a resident as private pay, but if the money runs out, they will allow conversion to Medicaid.

Mortgage Servicer: A company contracted to receive mortgage payments and handle the associated escrow account on behalf of a lender on a traditional forward mortgage. The company is designated to make disbursements to the borrower on a Reverse Mortgage and verify tax payments, insurance payments, and occupancy.

Non-Recourse Loan: A loan secured by collateral, which is the house in the case of a Reverse Mortgage. In the event of a default, the lender may only seize the collateral, even if its value does not satisfy repayment of the loan amount.

Note: A legal document indicating a promise to repay a loan along with all loan terms.

Paying off a Mortgage: This is a term commonly used by borrowers in ways that may not be technically correct. "Paying off a mortgage" in the context of a traditional mortgage means paying the balance to $0, but many borrowers also use the term when refinancing a mortgage. In the case of a refinance, the loan is not truly "paid off." Instead, a new loan replaces the old loan. When a Reverse Mortgage replaces any existing mortgage, the old loan is "paid off" and replaced by a new mortgage. If the new mortgage is a reverse, monthly payments to the lender become optional. See Eliminating a Mortgage Payment.

Power of Attorney (POA): A legal document allowing one person to act on behalf of another.

Primary Residence: The residence where someone lives most of the time. This is typically the residence reflected on a driver's license, tax returns, and voter registration.

Principal: The amount borrowed on a loan.

Principal Limit: The portion of a home's value that FHA will lend at closing with a Reverse Mortgage. It is based on borrower's age and the expected interest rate. It is adjusted over the life of the loan based on the actual interest rate and mortgage insurance rate. Details and the tables are available at <u>https://www.hud.gov/program_offices/housing/</u> <u>sfh/hecm.</u>

Tenure Payments: Guaranteed monthly payments made to a Reverse Mortgage borrower based on an FHA calculation of available Principal Limit and borrower age.

Term Payments: Payments made to a Reverse Mortgage borrower from the available Principal

Limit based on her specifications regarding amount and frequency.

Traditional (Forward) Mortgage: A home loan with a fixed or adjustable rate paid down by the borrower over a specified amount of time until the lender is repaid the entire balance. A good example would be the thirty-year fixed-rate mortgage that many people use to buy a home.